Bridging the Gulf

Bridging the Gulf

By ED GOULD

A Hilarious Look at Life on British Columbia's Gulf Islands

NEW REVISED AND EXPANDED EDITION

hancock house

ISBN-0-919654-35-5

PRINTED IN CANADA

Published by:

HANCOCK HOUSE PUBLISHERS
3215 Island View Road
Saanichton, British Columbia
Canada

DEDICATION

This book is dedicated to my wife, Jan, who encouraged me when the rains and the glooms came and who has always been my most honest and kind critic. It is also for my son Jason who has a much better sense of the ridiculous than I will ever have. And it is dedicated to the late Molly Townsend of Deep Cove, Vancouver Island, who typeset "Bridging The Gulf" in its first printing. If it hadn't been for Molly this second attempt wouldn't be here. Finally, this book is dedicated to the residents of the Gulf Islands. They are the finest people in the world and it was a privilege to be living among them.

Thanks are also extended to John Manning, publisher of the *Sidney Review*, for his kind permission in allowing portions of this book to be republished here.

Ed Gould has been a journalist most of his life and has worked for daily and weekly newspapers, radio and the national wire service. He was assistant editor of *The Victorian*, where he also wrote a popular column.

Prior to that he edited three Victoria area weeklies, was a reporter for *Victoria Times* and worked for various newspapers and radio stations in British Columbia and Alberta.

He now lives in Victoria where he is freelancing again, a pursuit he reluctantly gave up when he left the Gulf Islands. "No one ever really leaves the Gulf Islands," Mr. Gould said. "I go back frequently to visit friends and a half-acre lot there. The Gulf Islands never let you go."

Cartoons are by Nelson Dewey.

FOREWORD

The Gulf Islands used to be a haven for homesteaders, cattle-rustlers, sheep-stealers, persecuted persons and other who wanted to get away from the outside world.

American Negroes came here to set up homes in a new free land; survivors of the Klondike and Cariboo gold rushes dropped in after their "yellow fever" subsided.

The influx of retired folks, dreamers, poets, painters and artsy-crafties continues.

The attractions are many: gorgeous scenery, good climate, excellent fishing: trout and bass in the inland lakes and coho and spring salmon in the saltchuck.

Sailing enthusiasts enjoy cruising among hundreds of tiny, mainly uninhabited islands.

There's golf, horseback riding, hiking, sightseeing and swimming.

The main islands include Salt Spring, North and South Pender, Galiano, Gabriola, Saturna and Valdes—the latter suggesting some Spaniards got into the works somewhere along the line—which they did.

Don Juan Pantojay Arriaga, in the *San Carlos*, came on a survey assignment under the orders of the Viceroy of Mexico in 1791. He must have spoken well of the place because a year later Don Dionisio Alcala Galiano and Don Cayetano Valdes came to grab as much land and water as they could claim in the name of Spain.

The Spanish not only left their names behind, they cleared it with the Admiralty in Madrid that the air was fit to breathe.

Records show that the Islands were judged "pure and free of injuring gases"—a report that will doubtless be appreciated by those escaping industrial smells in less-favored parts of the continent.

No kidding. The sailors were provided with instruments called eudiometers to test for "malign vapors."

After the British went to the mat with the Spanish and won rights to the West Coast of Canada, they were disappointed to learn that salt springs on Salt Spring Island (unlike those of Banff or Radium Hot Springs) had no thermal value.

This must have enraged the British because the name of the island was changed to Admiralty Island, a change which the Islanders refused to accept. A habit of refusing to accept almost anything is characteristic of Gulf Islanders.

The few salt springs still burbling above the ground are, in fact, soundly cursed because the salt stains the lawns. A

Chamber of Commerce suggestion a few years ago to run a water pipe through a block of salt as a tourist attraction was met with a singular lack of enthusiasm.

The residents get more enthusiastic over genuine neighborly pursuits, like clam roasts. Legend has it that early Indians in the Islands were famous for their delicious roasted clams; one account says the Bella Bellas were roasting clams when Moses was writing the Pentateuch on Mount Sinai.

That prehistoric tourist industry never really got off the ground since invaders had their heads cut off with blunt axes, a custom which still has favor among some Island residents—although nowadays they just think about it.

However, some people actually did take the law into their own hands when oyster "burglars" in the form of commercial pickers began to strip the beaches clean of everything that would fit into a gunny sack.

There are still plenty of oysters and clams available. They really are best when they "r" in season, and visitors would be well-advised to check to see if the area involved is "posted" with a Fisheries Department warning. Pollution is not an unknown word in the Gulf Islands, unfortunately.

It is difficult to believe that such idyllic calmness now prevails where incredible hardships and bloody disputes took place one hundred years ago.

A bloodbath in Ganges Harbor between the Cowichans and Bella Bellas made the "tide run red"—according to an early account.

And then there is the famous battle of Maxwell Mountain in which rancher John Maxwell finally got tired of having his prime beef run off by renegade John McCawley (who came by way of New Westminster, B.C., and San Francisco) and his nefarious crew.

McCawley was finally ambushed by a small force of ranchers at Burgoyne Bay just as he was about to alight from a canoe filled with painted Cowichans.

The Indians, thinking McCawley had led them into a trap purposely, cut his throat and dumped his body in Sansum Narrows, a slim body of water that separates Salt Spring Island from Vancouver Island.

Two other Island skirmishes are worth noting: A Portugese gunboat once decided to have a target practice over "uninhabited" Pender Island until one of the "uninhabitants" complained to the British about cannon balls in his garden. The Portuguese were prevailed upon to desist.

The Pig War of 1859 was more serious and led to an

international incident which saw both British and American troops being dispatched to an island in the San Juans (the American Gulf Islands) where a porker had been shot.

The whole thing was settled amicably enough and not one shot was fired in anger. Save for the one that killed the pig.

An indirect result of the settling of the boundary dispute—which was largely behind the controversy—led to the Gulf Islands getting some more inhabitants: Hawaiians.

These Islanders had been settling in the San Juans since the early 1800s and many were related to the Kanakas, their Gulf Island equivalents. Many moved to the Canadian side of the border because they were used to a monarchial form of government and were leery of their rights under the republic.

Along about the same time, a number of Portugese jumped ship and swam to the Islands to help establish the cultural mosaic.

An amusing story about the Hawaiian contribution comes from Paul Roland of Isabella Point, Salt Spring. His grandfather, as tall and handsome a Hawaiian warrior as ever lived, told him about the time another old Kanakan was visited by a certain Mr. Cook, a resident of the Island.

"He thought he was related to Captain Cook," Mr. Roland said. "And you know what the Hawaiians did to him." (In case you don't—they ate him.)

"He fell down on his knees and said: 'Don't blame me, Captain Cook. I didn't eat your grandfather. I didn't even know him!'"

Another well-respected ethnic group on Salt Spring are the Negroes who came from United States during the Civil War and later. "Granny" Stark, a former plantation slave and matriarch of the black community until her death a few years ago, left behind an unpublished manuscript detailing some of the less serene incidents that took place on serene Salt Spring.

There are few disputes between Islanders today. Some Island businessmen were indirectly involved in an unfortunate hair-cutting incident known as the "Barbershop Quartet Caper" a few years ago. And meetings between North and South Galiano residents sometimes lead to occasional skirmishes behind the meeting hall. This is especially true if the

conversation turns to amalgamation, planning, incorporation, or anything that could be construed as an attempt to make Islanders conform.

This non-conformity manifests itself in unusual ways. A Fulford Harbour man once suggested that there were too many young people coming to the Islands and wanted them to be declared off-limits to anyone under 65. And one restaurant owner (now retired) suggested that merchants refuse to serve or sell food to "hippies", meaning anyone with long hair.

This did not have much affect on the young people who came here in droves a few years ago. Many have settled in small communes and are—for the most part—peaceful citizens of the Islands. Less welcome are the sheep rustlers who have been active, as notices pinned to bulletin boards indicate. Island dogs that run in packs are also a nuisance to sheep breeders, as are the occasional cougars that swim over from Vancouver Island.

Next to sheep-raising, tourism, fishing, logging, cattle-raising and fruit-farming are mainstays of the Islands' economies.

The animal population becomes apparent the moment you drive off the ferry. Cows, horses, sheep and even pigs wander at will across the highways and byways. Deer also are so tame they can present a pedestrian problem.

If you come by boat, watch out for the killer whales.

There have been few reports of these huge mammals up-setting boats, but they can upset the boaters as they cavort around their Chris-Crafts off South Pender Island. Stay calm and get out your camera. They'll never believe you back home otherwise.

Finding youreslf in a pod of whales can be pretty exciting, especially if you come along Haro Strait and the whales are in your lane!

The Islands are a photographer's dream. Most of the hilly, rocky areas are covered with greenery year-round. The arbutus tree (called Madrona in other parts of the coast) is the most familiar. It retains its large green leaves year-round but sheds its bark to reveal a deep, orange-green inter-ior. Colorful roadside gorse bushes display yellow springtime beauty.

Spelunking or cave-crawling is becoming a popular pastime. Maxwell Mountain—a heart-stopping two thousand foot viewpoint on Salt Spring—has several deep caverns you might try to find.

Other caves can be found on Galiano and Thetis. A less adventurous but equally appealing place of interest is the Malaspina Galleries on Gabriola Island, accessible by ferry from Nanaimo.

These natural etchings were carved into the sandstone by pounding sea and squirming prehistoric animals. Rockcollectors will find pebbles galore to pick, probe and preserve. Shops and stores in all communities have examples of crafts made locally. The Community Arts Councils and other organizations feature annual art fairs.

Skindivers enjoy the new provincial park, located at Beaver Point on Salt Spring, or any number of bays and inlets on South Pender. There are a number of ship wrecks that can be examined, including one named *Panther* which lies off Wallace Island between Salt Spring and Galiano. This ship went down 100 years ago; but don't expect gold—she was carrying coal.

The most famous Gulf Island event, known around the world, is its July First Lamb Barbecue. You haven't really enjoyed a simple, family outing unless you've been to Saturna on this day to celebrate Canada's birthday.

Everyone living on Saturna Island donates time and effort to make this outdoor feast a memorable event. Island lamb is barbecued over cedar-fed pits and served with salad and other dishes. Hundreds of boats tie up at Campbell Bay, tour boats come out from Victoria and the smell of lamb has been known to reach as far as Seattle, driving residents there mad with longing.

If you don't like your food burnt at the stake, you might prefer to frequent some of the small and quaint Old Country-style hotel restaurants. Like the Mayne Hotel, a former hostel for brick-workers, on Mayne Island. There's also Pender Island's Beauty Rest and Salt Spring's Harbor House (or Condor Inn, as it is now called).

There are three nine-hole golf courses on the Islands— Salt Spring, Galiano and North Pender. And they are seldom crowded. Perhaps they are being used at night. The Salt Spring has long been the sighting spot for Unidentified Flying Objects.

Another good reason to vacation on the Gulf Islands. The "aliens" may be getting ready to take over!

After "Bridging The Gulf" was first published I was be-
sieged by people (who didn't live on the Gulf Islands) about
what sort of reaction the Islanders would have. Some felt
that the picture I had painted was not exactly flattering. I
wasn't trying to be flattering, I was trying to write something
that would amuse. And I felt I accomplished this because the
most enthusiastic readers were those who make the Gulf Islands their home year-round.

They weren't all flatterers, mind you. Some were just
puzzled. Like the man at Hope Bay on North Pender Island.
He was a big man, about two hundred and fifty pounds, who
looked like a sea captain gone to seed. On his head he had a
very greasy captain's hat, riddled with holes. His brownish

shirt was knotted just above his belly button and between there and his pants—held up by rope—was an expanse of very red stomach.

When he spoke his mouth twitched on one side and this was in exact opposition to one eye which ticced along on another beat. His pants were ripped off in a jag at the knees and his feet, knobbly and covered with scars and warts, were bare.

"Tell me," he said, eye ticcing, mouth twitching, belly undulating, "where the hell did you dream up the characters you got in that book of yours?"

Gulf Islanders are a composite of the real and the imaginary. But any characters or incidents in this book are, unless specifically identified otherwise, to be considered fictional and though the dividing line between fiction and reality sometimes becomes difficult to distinguish, there is no intention to wound or malign actual persons, living or dead.

Another example of someone taking things too seriously was graphically pointed out to me one day when a friend, Steve Clinehens, who was then living with his wife and baby on tiny Adland Island, came triumphantly into our Salt Spring Island home brandishing a newspaper clipping.

"I see you made it in the *Times*," he said.

"I've made it a lot in the *Times*," I replied. "I'm on a retainer for them."

"No, no," Clinehens said, "I don't mean the *Victria Times*. I mean the *New York Times*!"

I couldn't believe it. Something I had written had been picked up by Canadian Press, the wire service that circulates news to Canadian dailies. Associated Press in United States had picked up the item from CP and the *New York Times* had picked it up from there.

It all began with a spoof piece I wrote about the mink that were then proliferating along the shores of the Gulf Islands.

The story, as published in the *Victoria Times,* said that "mink are getting so tame and numerous on Salt Spring Island they'll walk up and eat right out of your hand." The second paragraph warned however: "After you've had the doctor stitch all your fingers back on, you'll remember that man's best friend is still a dog."

The wire service story didn't bother to reveal the spoof inherent in the second paragraph and so it appeared as a straight news story in the *New York Times.* "Minks Become Bold On Canadian Island", the headline read.

I often wondered, what with the price of mink and the gullibility of some New Yorkers about life in the "frozen wastelands" of Canada, if a few didn't come up here and try to catch mink by hand.

The best of luck to them! And to you, dear reader. Have fun.

ED GOULD
Victoria, British Columbia

Chapter One

THE RIGORS OF THE GOOD LIFE

"Come and enjoy the good life with us," they said.
But they forgot to mention that we had to provide it first.

Our first visit to the Gulf Islands will be long-remembered. Even if most of the wounds *do* heal.

It was Fred and Mabel Fergus who got us there; they'd been extolling the pleasures of the Islands for years: "Trees full of ripe fruit just waiting to be picked," they said. "Clams and oysters waiting to be scooped off the beach."

What we didn't know was that all the picking and scooping was to be done by us.

We had visualized that we would spend our days cruising the Islands in one of those expensive, flying poop deck boats;

our evenings would be spent relaxing with a gin and tonic on a veranda overlooking the tranquil ocean.

There was no veranda on the Fergus shack. It did not overlook the ocean. It stared into a few trees at the end of a cow pasture.

"Don't you just love the view," Mabel gushed. To see it you had to stand on the toilet seat and crane your neck out a tiny cracked window. All I got was a crick in the crack.

The Fergus site was situated near the top of a mountain, farther inland than Cranbrook. It was obtainable by following a rutted, dusty trail that offered mudholes, sandtraps, quagmires and sharp stones to the car tires. We arrived there hot and dusty and had already forgotten our pleasant ferry ride over from Vancouver.

The dust was still settling into our hair and clothing when Mabel suggested we might like to pick a few blackberries "before dark." It was four o'clock in the afternoon.

However, *everything* was dark, including my humor, when we returned from the prickle patch. We were stung by insects, dropped on by birds, endangered by bulls and pulled apart by thorns. Jan, my wife, had stepped in something.

But we had enough blackberries to keep the Fergus larder full all winter.

I was almost sitting down when Fred mentioned fresh cool apple juice. I was out of my crouch (from getting at the low branches) in a flash, only to learn that Fred meant we had to make the stuff first.

We spent an hour pulping apples into a wooden barrel. While he wasn't looking, I spiked his grog with a few windfall stinkers.

After a spartan breakfast consisting of corn flakes, skim milk and the more over-ripe fruits of the previous day's labor, we struck off for the beach, ten miles downhill. Fred showed me how to crack oysters but the pain that shot up my arm indicated that it was my wrist and not the oyster shell that had cracked.

Owing to my incapacitated right arm, Fred cut short the quest for crustaceans and offered to drive my car back up the mountain. "I always wanted to drive one of these Jap jobs," he said. First, we crammed the trunk full of sandy, salt-soaked driftwood. One hour and a punctured oil pan later we arrived to find the ladies stealing apples from an old orchard below the Fergus menage.

"Get the high ones," Fred yelled from below. "They're *all* high," my wife said, just before the rotten branch she was standing on gave way and dumped her face down into a clump of rose bushes.

"Rose hips are an excellent source of vitamin C," Mabel cried. My wife cried a little too.

Later, as we sat in front of the fire that I had cut the kindling for, Fred regaled us with stories of how other friends had been conned into helping stock their freezer and woodshed.

"Sam Thompson got sunstroke and couldn't eat a mouthful of the twenty-eight pound Coho he caught," Fred laughed. We hadn't been able to do justice to the meal that evening either. I don't know whether it was the fish poisoning in my arm or just Mabel's cooking that made my body throb all over. It did seem to me that the main vegetable was some sort of weed.

"It must be edible," Mabel said, as everyone sat looking at the stuff steaming on our plates. "It grew in our back garden." My wife said later that she had't noticed anything edible growing there. She should know. She had to weed it before dinner

Lying in bed that night, staring up from the lump of the mattress, we decided to give up the good life for the time being and escape to the comfort of our own home.

But the spell of the Islands had left its mark. We were to return many times before finally deciding to move there ourselves.

The first year we lived on the Islands we still couldn't get over the abundance of everything. Pretty soon we were sending out letters to friends and relatives:

"You reallly ought to come over some time and partake of Nature's bounty," we wrote. "Trees full of ripe fruit just waiting to be picked. . . ."

CHAPTER TWO
A SPANIARD IN THE WORKS

*In which it is revealed that a Spanish legacy
remains salty to this day.*

When the Spaniards discovered the Gulf Islands they
noticed right away that the largest island in the group was
dotted with fresh water springs. Being rather sneaky sorts,
the Spanish called the place Salt Spring Island, thus keeping
the British, French and Portugese away from their watering
holes for years.

The British eventually caught on to this shell game and
began a shell game of their own. They pumped shells into the
Spanish ships until they wouldn't hold *any* water and the
Spaniards were forced to withdraw from Salt Spring.

They also withdrew from Galiano, Saturna, Valdes,
Cortes, Quadra and Turner Valley, Alberta, leaving nothing

behind but their names, a foraign address, and a lot of little children who tended to lisp in a Castillian way.

The only Island along the coast that the Spanish did not leave was the only one that they did not conquer—Mayne island. The Spaniards wouldn't touch Mayne with a ten-foot pole, so it lay undiscovered until the arrival of Walter Maynski, a 10-foot Pole from Winnipeg.

For the uninitiated, the Gulf Islands are roughly located in the Gulf of Georgia (which is not a gulf at all but a strait and is 5,864 miles northwest of Georgia. Who says the Spanish were the only sneaky explorers?) right under the soft underbelly of Vancouver Island.

The major centre of all the Inner and Outer Islands is a village called Ganges, named after a ship. The ship was named after the famous holy river in India. Which may account for the East Indians who worked in the sawmills on Vancouver Island coming over to wash their holy socks in Ganges Harbor.

Historians say that Salt Spring has a motley background (mainly because the historians were Bert and Ethel Motley). Its first non-Indian residents were black settlers who came from the United States to escape persecution. Waiting here to persecute them were the Indians. And the cougars and bears. However, the cougars and bears did not like the Indians either, so it can hardly be claimed that they based their prejudice on color.

Next to arrive was the Englishman, escaping persecution, high taxes, high blood pressure, and a nagging wife in south London. Typically, the English first took out title to all the land so everything was neat and legal before the first shot was fired to protect these rights.

These settlers found the land on the Gulf Islands to be extremely fertile and capable of supporting large crops of vegetables, fruits and children. Without any assistance from the government (there was no government anyway), these hardy types soon zoomed the population to three thousand souls, mostly unsaved.

The church soon put a stop to that. Or tried. It established churches, schools and itinerant preachers. But the Islanders were proud of their ignorance and were ready to fight for it to the last unwashed man, woman and child.

Their resistance was eventually broken when tourists began to arrive to take pictures and the Canadian Broadcasting Corporation called them quaint. The Islanders called the CBC types "queer" in defence.

But the quaintness of the natives has some basis in fact. For example, the current topic of conversation around the docks, general stores and swimming pools revolves around the miraculous wrack and ruin of Paddy Mack.

Paddy was born, raised and uneducated on Pender Island. He courted but never married. His social life consisted of rowing, his washing tied to the back of the boat, to Prevost Island, drying it on a rock, and rowing back.

Recently, however, the tide has turned for Paddy Mack. (To say nothing for what it's done to his socks and underwear.) At the age of 76, Paddy made his first trip off the Island with a bargeload of other old age pensioners who went seeking wine, women, and pension cheque increases and songs at the Silver Threads Centre in Victoria.

He returned with a bicycle and an Eaton's catalogue. But Paddy's life is irrevocably changed. He is already talking about acquiring a washing machine and his friends are worried about how far this lunacy will extend.

This "lunacy" may in fact be spreading—so be cautious. They are saying now that people who visit the Gulf Islands fall under a spell and tend to become lazy and dreamy. And not all of them smoke those funny cigarettes.

I don't believe it. And after living on and off the Islands for eight years, I can honestly say I have not become a Lotus Eater.

The reason for this beard and generally unkempt appearance is simply because I have not been able to get any regular employment at my own profession.

There doesn't seem to be much call for journeymen nit-pickers anymore.

CHAPTER THREE
AS HE BREWS, SO SHALL HE DRINK

Eat, drink and be merry, for tomorrow
may be Saturna.

It has long been suspected that people select their favorite Gulf Island to settle on because of the drinking habits of that particular Island. That suspicion has now been confirmed.

According to the crew of the *Queen of the Islands* (the B.C. Ferries ship that goes everywhere but to Saturna), the drinking customs go something like this:

Rowdy passengers reel off at Mayne; hale and hearty, do-it-yourself-and-hang-the-cost-types spring off at Galiano; farmers and male pensioners creep off at Pender and old ladies of both sexes fall out at Salt Spring.

This is gross simplification, and therefore probably half true. After all, Mayne Islanders should not *all* be classified as beer-guzzlers. In addition to numerous six-packs of lager and pilsener, I have personally observed many brawny Mayne arms hugging paper bags clinking-full of ale and stout.

The ferrymen contend it's always more peaceful aboard after the Mayneliners have been unloaded at Village Bay but to further claim that the sea actually becomes calmer is exaggeration. It is a scientific fact, however, that the wind tends to drop rather dramatically.

It's also unfair to infer that Salt Spring has nothing but old ladies living on it. There are a lot of old men living there too. The sherry-drinking rule is true, however. Because of it, Salt Spring Island has gained a reputation as one of the quietest places on earth.

Unlimited amounts of inexpensive sherry are offered each afternoon around four o'clock when the sun is hottest so that everone is in the sack with a splitting headache around seven-thirty.

A case can also be made for the scotch-drinking that goes on in little bungalows and quiet shacks on the twin Pender Islands. Here, male pensioners, remittance men and old soldiers who never dry, live in reduced circumstances. They may not live well, but they live *high*.

Someone (I hope) may have noticed that Saturna has been left out of this revelation. Saturna is left out of everything except their July First lamb barbeque. They even took away its free school. However, the ferrymen are sure of one thing: Saturnans usually make their own ferry connections, are home-brew addicts and hold only one major holiday of their own, July Second.

It is on this day that Saturnans hold a Saturnalia to thank Bacchus for sending all those beer-guzzling lamb-eaters to Campbell Bay on Dominion Day.

The main reason that residents of the Outer Islanders carry home their booze on anything that will float is because selfish Salt Spring has the only legal grog shop, the government liquor store in Ganges. For non-Salt Springers, it's either get loaded up internally and externally there (or in Sidney) or rely on bootleggers and weekend rumrunners.

"Comin' out Saturday, Sam? Bring some beer, two bottles of V.O., a Captain Morgan and a mickey of Gordon's gin. Oh yeah . . . bring something for the Jungle Mouth. The wife's singin' in the choir on Sunday."

Being totally teetotal, the Galiano Water Diviners view all this battle for the bottle with disdain. They have made it known that they would prefer watery graves to fire water.

This is only true of the Southenders where the booze cruisers never dock. The Northenders have been known to take a drop or two. Take the incident where two of their number recently ended up at the lockup. Drunk charges were laid against them for being three sheets to the wind (with another luffing badly). The guard told me that they were so full of beer that he had to take two inches off the doorjam to get them into the cell.

In light of the ferrymen's analyses of Island drinking traditions, it is not difficult to understand why Galiano has two distinct groups whose views are at opposite ends of the liquor pole.

If you take a look at a map of Galiano, you'll notice it's long and skinny. The Island is also slowly separating into two separate pieces of land.

One way or another, the Southenders are moving to disown the North!

CHAPTER FOUR
CANDLELIGHT AND WHINE

*A breakdown of current values in which it is demonstrated
that the key to beautiful entertainment on the Gulf Islands
may be in the eye of the hurricane.*

Where was Moses when the lights went out? You've all
heard that old joke. The answer is: he was in the dark. And
probably on the Gulf Islands.

All it takes to ensure a power failure on the Gulf Islands
is to hold a party, get engrossed in a good book or television
program, or lay in a winter's supply of frozen meat.

More people dine by candlelight on the Gulf Islands than
all the lovers in Rome and Paris laid end to end. Candlelight
services are held in Gulf Island churches year-round, not just
during Holy Days. Without candles to light the way, the faithful would fall on their faces instead of their knees.

The big winds that patrol these waters are the culprits in this power play. The winds are also the control factor in what programs are watched on television.

Giant Douglas firs have been known to stand fast during seventeen Lucy reruns but fall flat across the powerline halfway through Masterpiece Theatre or Hockey Night In Canada.

Consequently, these periods of darkness, known as the Dark Ages locally because it seems like ages that you're in the dark, have forced whole families to fall back on old-fashioned entertainment.

Grandfather terrifies the baby by wiggling his knobby old joints in front of a candle and producing grotesque shadowgraphs on the wall. Adult jaws work slowly and awkwardly unfamiliar two-syllable words as the full horror of live conversation is thrust upon them.

Men who haven't spoken one hundred words to their wives in two years suddenly find themselves yelling twenty and thirty words to the minute: "Where are the candles? Who moved the flashlight? Get that cat out of here!"

Girls croon lullabyes to their dolls to keep up their courage while little brother wait in darkened hallways to push them down the stairs.

One South Pender mother took advantage of the blackness. She left home for three days. When she returned the power outage was still on; no one knew she'd been away. She's praying for another big wind to come. She won't have long to wait.

The favorite entertainment however is the guessing game about how long the power will be off. It has largely replaced, for ex-Prairie people at least, the Springtime betting match on when the ice will go out on the river.

As the bets come in for whether it will be a long or short power outage, other odds are calculated: will it be worth going out to the shed and bringing in the sleeping bags, hurricane lamps and camp stove? Or should they remain hopeful and hold on for a little while longer?

The hopefuls (known sometimes as the lazies) usually find themselves waiting, cold and sore, until the sun comes up and the power comes on.

Business continues to function on the Islands regardless of power failures. Taxi drivers carry chain saws in their trunks so they can cut their way through the fallen logs to their passengers' homes. One Galiano driver claims he's never yet lost a passenger to a tree.

Surely the most frustrating and costly result of the blackouts is the mess in the frozen food chest. High-priced meat gets even higher after it's thawed a few times.

The most resourceful man in the Gulf Islands was the Salt Springer on Beddis Road who decided that his huge fish supply was in jeopardy because of a particularly long power cut.

A veteran skindiver, he donned his wetsuit to disgorge the freezer of its sloppy, slippery inhabitants. After getting them all safely into the back seat of his Volkswagen for a hasty ferry trip to a friend's place in Sidney, the light came on again. Every light—including last year's Christmas string, which wasn't even hooked up.

This poignant moment best exemplifies the attitude of the Islanders towards the powers that won't be at B.C. Hydro and Awfully Powerful.

Although they fervently believe that everything comes to he who waits, why must it always be in the dark?

Let there be light!

CHAPTER FIVE
A CRABBY COCKTAIL

*Not since the Gathering of the Clams has so much been
owed to so few by so many.*

There are two or three nights during the year when the
tides are extremely low that are best for Gulf Island crab-
grabbing. Unfortunately—and even before pollution des-
troyed the best crab grounds—the crabs were well aware of
these two or three nights.

They usually planned to be elsewhere when the time
came for the hopeful novice to come out with pole and bucket
to try to collect their pink, young bodies.

The annual Giant Crab Hunt at Fulford Harbor was a
complete washout the year we attended.

The hunt was to be held on a Saturday night. The other
fifty-odd revellers were to meet us at the Fulford beach after

hoisting a few at a friend's place first. We were so late we went directly to the crabbing area.

It was 10 p.m. and full moon. The tidal flats lay naked for nearly a mile. Then the moon waxed, waned and withered and the weather became what the meteorologists call "unseasonal". Unreasonable would be better: petty, irrational, unpredictable and generally ill-mannered.

One minute it was almost balmy. The next minute so were we. It went from squally to sleet to frigid. Not at all like the advance notices we'd been given about weather for the Giant Crab Hunt.

At last, some of the more hardy souls that had been weathering it indoors arrived. They were quite well weathered and spent most of their time laughing and trying to get into each other's clothes.

Dress was as varied as the persons wearing it. The crusty crustaceans were about to advance before a horde of hoary Islanders in everything from oilskins to bare skins. With the weather changing every few minutes, the ideal gear appeared to be a fur-lined jock strap and a pair of gumboots.

Those of us who actually left the beach, where car lights were left on, started across the muck of the flats, puncturing the night with our flashlights and joyful cries: "Hey, here's something!" "It's an octopus!" "Ugh!" "I'm sinking!" "Save me!" And similar fun phrases.

Through the slime, seaweed, sludge and odd parts of metal that had fallen off myriad boats over the years, the splattered crew slithered.

A half dozen crabs were actually found and captured. My wife tested the claws of one to determine whether they really were as strong as reported. They were. Her testing finger turned a determined blue.

Later, under the welcoming blaze of a shoreline bonfire, some of the deep creepers were boiled in pots of steaming sea water. While the crabs were getting boiled, some Islanders were getting the same way, by a different, internal heating process.

Before the crabs were ready to be eaten, and just prior to Jan's finger turning black, it began to snow. It *never* snows on the Gulf Islands—particularly during the Giant Crab Hunt.

We returned to our car with empty buckets, full boots, empty stomachs and empty heads.

We were, nevertheless, crabby.

CHAPTER SIX
NO NUDES IS GOOD NUDES

*The troops hit the beaches and get a charge out of the
enemy.*

There have been reports of hairy hippies strolling hand-in-hand with naked nymphs along the sandy beaches of the Gulf Islands. Eyebrows were raised.

According to one informant, the raising distance of the eyebrows was far exceeded by that attained by popping eyeballs.

A vigilantes group was formed to run the nudeniks off the Islands; there were lots of eager volunteers.

It all began when a few beer-drinking youngsters decided to go swimming in the buff. The police got wind of it and a plan of action was decided upon almost before the first pair of briefs hit the sand.

"It was awful," one of the volunteers told me, his eyes glazing over at the recollection. "Buncha naked girls running around without a stitch on, right here on a public beach."

The police had asked that volunteers help handle the situation. Although they had difficulty before in whipping up enthusiasm for fighting bush fires, small floods and other disasters, they had no trouble at all in recruiting for this civil defence exercise.

Old veterans unable the previous week to raise more than a foaming beer in their own defence, now found sudden vitality and sprang from behind their tables to rush to the country's needs.

Under one old ex-Captain's command, the force quickly assembled at a vantage point on a sand dune above the action. By now, about fifty young men and women were singing in the sea and frolicking in the fronds in their birthday suits.

The commandos synchronized their watches, adjusted their bifocals and—with a hoarse cry of "Charge!" from their leader—hit the beach.

The battle was soon over and cries of victory came from the volunteers as they herded the dazed nudies into a circle near a large, well-stoked bonfire.

Some old chaps expressed regret that they hadn't been able to get to the front before the action was over. They'd had to be content at flailing their crutches at retreating backs and sides.

But their disappointment was lessened somewhat when they were allowed to form an unblinking phalanx along the route to the police truck.

Despite the size of the operation, there were no serious injuries, except for two vets who suffered a rare type of ailment diagnosed as Buff Man's Blind. It's caused when human eyes are held open without blinking for more than an hour at a time.

"You won't miss anything even if you do blink occasionally," the eye specialist told the sufferers later.

There were some complaints among those arrested. One robusty maiden objected to the way the big pinch was conducted. She said the girls had nothing but the steamy glances of their captors to cover them until their clothes arrived—in a separate truck—at the police station an hour later.

The community fathers, meanwhile, were gratified at the swift action of the police and volunteers at nipping nudism in the bud.

Some of the volunteers, veterans of the Boer War, said it was the greatest rearguard action since the seige of Mafeking in 1899.

CHAPTER SEVEN
NO SIGN OF SIGNS

Gulf Islanders will sign anything, except beaches.

Signs play a large part in the way of life on the Gulf Islands. They lead the way to motels, resorts, public campgrounds. They lead to everything but beaches.

An exasperated tourist on Pender Island complained he had spent two full days and a fruitless night searching for a public beach. People kept telling him, "just follow the signs." There were signs all along the way, but they finally led nowhere.

On Mayne Island they don't lead tourists astray like that. They don't lead them at all. Signs are forbidden on Mayne and the natives like it that way. It's well-known that outsiders have driven into Bennett Bay looking for a way to get off the Island.

Some people settled on Mayne Island because they couldn't find their way off. Others stayed because they couldn't find the tree blazes that led to the beach where they'd left their boats.

Even residents have a hard time finding the beaches. We once looked for a highly recommended beach on Salt Spring. Signs drew us all the way from Ganges but died within shouting distance of the beach near Beddis Park. We kept ending up at a deadend road, a rocky pinnacle four hundred feet above sea level.

We had the choice of contemplating the setting sun or observing the bird droppings in the tops of the Douglas Firs below us.

We finally found the beach after a third attempt. You reach it by driving through a gate across what is cleverly disguised to look like a cow pasture.

We asked one of the residents nearby what happened to the beach sign.

"How would you like to have a bunch of unwashed kids shouting and drowning next to *your* house?" he asked.

We took our kid home and washed him in rain water.

There are other signs of the times on the Gulf Islands: A veterinarian, now deceased, had a sign proclaiming he would train sheep dogs. On the very same sign post was another that warned of the dire penalties that would be inflicted on any wool-picking dog caught molesting sheep.

Near Beaver Point there are signs telling you to beware of a pet deer and a dozen hand-lettered signs prohibiting shooting because of "grazing horses." The owner of the horses claims quite rightly that his horses were being grazed by bullets of hunters who couldn't tell a horse from a hyena.

A St. Mary Lake oldtimer had a sign on his property that told everyone: "Tresspassing by appointment only" and another sign at Southey Point, also on Salt Spring, says: "Watch for children. No shooting."

Cat lovers are prevalent on the Gulf Islands, and one resident on Old Scott Road on Salt Spring posted a sign asking drivers to please watch out for them. A friend, who hates cats, said he always does. "But they're always too darned fast for me."

Chapter Eight
PRAIRIES ARE FOR CHICKENS

A Flat Earth policy is discovered behind this fowl plot.

"The Gulf Islands used to be populated with nothing but good, native-born, fourth-generation Englishmen," the real estate man told me.

"Now we're being flooded with all kinds of Americans, foreigners and Prairie Chickens."

"Prairie Chickens?" I asked.

"Yeah. Prairie Chickens. Tough old birds from the Prairie Provinces. You can always tell a Prairie Chicken just by what he wants in the way of a place to retire to."

"Once a Chicken client of mine bought a lot over on Mayne Island. Then he wanted to know how much it would cost to cut down the trees and level the land. He said he couldn't see the view for the hills and trees!

"Yes, sir. It's sure hard to sell to a Prairie Chicken."

"Well," I said, "what do you do for them then? Sell them a piece of waterfront or view property they don't want?"

"Heck, no," the realtor answered. "We got ethics. Sometimes I sell them a piece of interior island as far away from the water as possible where they can clear off all the trees.

"Then they can build a little shack on a hill away from the view and into the wind. Prairie Chickens seem to love the wind. If I haven't got a suitable property I bulldoze a piece of good, hilly land, drain off a lake and put up a few strands of barbed wire."

"I guess that's no different than the B.C. sea captain who married a Saskatchewan girl and moved to the Prairies," I said. "He built himself a house like a ship with portholes instead of windows. Then he got his hired man to walk around at night and slosh a pail of water against the sides of the house so he'd feel right at sea."

"That's an isolated example," the real estate salesman pouted. "Here's a typical type for you. A painter from Red Deer bought a whole twenty acres of waterfront on Pender Island. He cleared out the centre like a gopher's dream.

"Then he built a big, rambling house with a veranda all around it and a sunporch overlooking two old outhouses. He sits in one of them with the door shut and paints pretty pictures all day."

"Sounds like a pretty good adjustment to me," I said.

"Oh yeah? He paints pictures of crocuses and snow fences. The only time he sees his million dollar view is when he goes hunting and the game takes off for the cliffs.

"I could subdivide that waterfrontage into quarter-acre lots and make a fortune. It's a criminal waste."

"Surely there are *some* Prairie people who like a view and take to water," I said. "They can't all suffer from hydrophobia."

"A Prairie Chicken only likes water in a slough, full of alkali, with a barn on one side full of ducks and geese," the man said. "Too much water in one place reminds him of floods and Saturday night bath water."

"Well," I said, "why do they come here then? There are lots of other flat, dry places to retire to."

"They like the weather. It's mostly good the year 'round. And there are a lot of other Chickens living here now that they can get together with and yap about how cold it is back in Gravelbourg."

"Sounds ideal, all right," I agreed. "Maybe after a while they'll settle right in and become typical Gulf Islanders."

"No chance," the realtor said. "I practically raised a Chicken who moved to Victoria twenty years ago. She finally saved enough money to buy her dream home. I sold her most of an island for a song. Know what she did with it? Cleared it like a plate, stuck a two-storey house on it with a veranda running around on both levels.

"Then she built a red barn, put in a dozen chickens and a bull calf and invited all her relatives and friends to visit what she called her Island Paradise. She might just as well have been in Ponoka."

The salesman suddenly looked carefully at me.

"Say . . . where'd you say you were from?"

"Southwest of Calgary."

"Well listen," he said. "I've got a lovely piece of waterfront on Galiano Island that's just come on the market. It faces south so you get all the sun and you can see all the ships and ferries go by day and night. Want to go look at it?"

"Well . . ." I said, "I was just wondering. Do you maybe have something a bit back of the water. You know . . . a couple of outbuildings. Fenced, not too many trees?"

CHAPTER NINE
ROCK ISLAND GRAFFITI AND THE
SILVER MENACE

*In which Gurg and Toad are threatened, but
nothing is said of the Crutch Crickets.*

A silver-tipped brusher may be systematically destroying authentic native-writing on Salt Spring Island rock faces.

We are not talking here of your Indian petroglyphs as written about in Ray and Beth Hill's book. These are rock-writings of a more recent nature.

The discovery that they are endangered was made by the Gulf Islands Graffiti and Clam-Lettering Society, a group whose purpose is to protect a long tradition of rock-carving and tree-painting.

The midnight skulker with the paint pot and brush has already cut a swath through some outstanding examples of native wit and wisdom and the Society is worried for the safety of Gurg and Toad. These two works of art are to be seen on rock faces at the corner of Scott and old Scott Roads on Salt Spring Island.

Society members are concerned lest "Long Live Crutch Crickets" (near Quebec Drive), will be covered with a thick coat of silver, the fate that smothered "Keep out corn-plaster."

On the Gulf Islands, as elsewhere, you'll discover "Grads 73", "Grads 74", "Grads 75", but where else will you find "Grads '07"; and where indeed, "Down with Flab"?

A few "Fred loves Toots" tend to ruin the tone of the more enterprising "Scratch and Live", found near the Long Harbor ferry wharf, but this is more than compensated for by the warning, in translucent white paint: "The Queen of the Islands is a ferry!"

The main question we are concerned with today, how-ever, is the awful implications behind the recent obliteration of some historical rock messages. A current theory is that the silver-painting may be a backlash generated by a frustrated group of rock-writers.

Remember a few years ago when you could drive be-tween Victoria and Campbell River and read most of the New Testament written in white paint on rocks and trees? No re-ligious cult was quite so rocal (the same as vocal, but in a rock vein). To them, every stone was a Rock of Ages. Every day Moses came down from the Mount with a fresh tablet.

Later on, someone went about writing irreverencies un-der the message: "Jesus Saves." A favorite was "Green Stamps"—or worse: "Beer Bottles."

The religious writers finally gave up and peace returned to the highways. However, the theory is that this group has reformed, called itself the Rock Rollers, and is out to destroy all rock-writings created by other groups.

The Graffiti Society is talking of posting twenty-four hour watches to guard their collection. A sort of rock-around-the-clock. It's their concern that the Rock Rollers intend to push their silver brushes right across the landscape. The situation is tense.

In the words of the Society president, "nothing seems sacred to those rotten _†+‡•£%&!!"

Chapter Ten
CATS, RATS AND OTHER DOGGONE ANIMALS

There's more than one way to skin a rat and keep a hungry hound from your door.

Gulf Islanders are excessively devoted to animals. Human beings they tolerate, but animals they love.

There was a lady living in Fulford Harbor who had to leave her home because neighbors (and her landlord) objected to the fourteen foot high fence she wanted to have constructed to keep her fifty-seven cats at home at night.

Some people just have no toleration.

But the most devoted animal lover (aside from the Salt Spring lady whose cats and goats keep her warm in the house) is the old man on Saturna who owned a huge, brown

colorèd dog of doubtful ancestry which had an appetite like a horse and feet to match.

The dog's master had a sign painted that warned strangers to beware. It wasn't that he was afraid the dog would bite anybody. He just didn't want him to kick them to death. He also smelled. Like a beached whale in the hot sun.

As with all men (and a great deal of women), death came. In his will the old chap left the dog to his grandson and his wife, who lived in Vancouver.

The story went that the grandson had been buttering-up to the old man, hoping to get his valuable waterfront property on Saturna. Instead, he got the dog. They were not overjoyed.

The couple then repaired to Vancouver to lick their wounds and calculate their losses.

The day of reckoning came and the youg couple visited Saturna and took delivery of the beast from the old man's faithful housekeeper who had stayed on in the house.

About a month went by.

The old housekeeper missed the big horse of a dog, especially on those nights when the wind blew in from the southeast, the trees trembled and the fog rolled right up to the windows.

One night the wind reached a fever pitch and in its fury, hurled a two hundred foot Douglas Fir across a power line right in the midst of the old housekeeper's favorite television program, "The Waltons".

An eerie silence followed. The wind had dropped and you could hear a leaf drop outside the house. There came a feeble scratching sound outside the kitchen door.

Heart in her mouth, tears in her eyes, the little old lady shuffled forth, flickering candle in hand, to let in the faithful hound she felt sure was waiting outside.

"Bless his $2.97-a-pound beef-eating heart," she whispered.

The door squeeked open. And there, lying on the doorstep in a pathetic heap, were the grandson and his wife. They had crawled all the way from Vancouver.

The dog had eaten them out of house and home!

Chapter Eleven
A DRIVING URGE

*In which it is shown that Gulf Island driving ranges from
Le Mans to Le Womans. Or: If at first you don't
succeed, back up and try again.*

All you sports car racing fans who haven't got the money
or time to drive great distances to the annual automobile
bashes at Indianapolis, Siebring or LeMans can always join
driving sports on the Gulf Islands.

The lack of the roaring crowds and the smell of the
grease pits (or is it the smell of the crowds and the roar of
grease pits?) is more than made up for by the chance you have
to compete in the race.

Here on the Islands you can match driving skills with
the Salt Springers (Leaf and Coil), the Pender Fender Bend-
ers and the Mayne Mainliners. To say nothing of the Galiano
Cargoyles, a ladies' group.

See them all demonstrate their unique style, born partly of local conditions and partly of a natural flair for being different.

Politically, the residents of the Gulf Islands are like anywhere else in British Columbia: they swing from left to right. But when it comes to driving, Gulf Islanders are unswervingly center of the road.

With the exception of Salt Spring, which has a white line on its main highway (often used as a single lane by motorcyclists), most of the Islands have one unlined ribbon of pavement and tributaries of gravel, dirt and sheep tracks.

Sheep, incidentally, which run wild on most Islands, are accorded the same pedestrian privileges accorded to humans: none.

It is perhaps unfair to say that all vehicles travel the centre line. One vehicle does go up the right side and down the left. It's the road grader—a non-resident on many Islands—which is given the privilege of scraping the gravel off the pitted surfaces once a year, whether the road needs it or not.

The average driver is not restricted as the grader is. He can pass on the side closest and most convenient at the time of meeting another vehicle, usually at the top of a hill.

Pender Islanders, of both North and South persuasion, boldly hug the centre of the road, bridge and mountain trail. A tourist can be identified as the clawing individual with the purple face on the edge of the hairpin turn, car balancing on air currents above the inlet one hundred feet below.

Another Island trait is an unlicensed attitude towards cars. That is, licences are considered an unnecessary luxury or inconvenience.

During a visit to one of the smaller Outer Islands I watched one woman retrieve her licenceless car from the bush where it had been hidden from the Mounties looking for such licenceless cars.

The woman informed me that she had been on a pinnacle with binoculars all the previous week watching for the police to make their annual snoop swoop.

A modernized version of the moccasin telegraph informed other residents of the Island to abandon and camoflage their vehicles until the cops had left.

At least there is one compensation about driving on the Gulf Islands which you will not find elsewhere: you always get a friendly wave just before the crash.

Not since Charles De Gaulle became a Quebec Libra has Canada had such a response to a two-fingered salute. Your average city driver, travelling life's highway via the cynic route, is upset by such unexpected friendliness. He doesn't quite know what to do when an Islander instinctively welcomes him with a two-digit wave, neither of which is placed alongside, or on the nose.

Actually, the two-finger salute is only a remainder of the friendliness of a happier day when a full-armed flail greeted *each* passing car.

Too bad, but the trend has already begun to drop even the two-finger wave. Lately, a one-finger flip is all you get, and this token recognition is being misunderstood by foreigners from Eastern Canada and Vancouver.

Remember how that comedian, Jackie Amson, was kicked off the old Ed Sullivan television show for improperly waving a Churchillian V? The angle of the dangle makes all the difference.

At any rate, before even the two-finger wave disappears the challenge of the roads is still there—as long as the Islanders fight off any attempt to connect them with Vancouver Island through a series of bridges.

Just in case it happens, and you then will have to drive all the way to Indianapolis, better book a passage now on the ferry.

Chapter Twelve
BAREFOOT IN WHALES

*In which it is clearly demonstrated that poor equipment
and sailing fishermen should stay
on common ground.*

When the local fish expert on Pender Island offered to take me out where the big ones were, I naturally thought he meant salmon.

But we ended up on killer whale alley!

However, my ignorance of fishing knows no bounds. I was brought up on the "bent pin" school of fishing techniques and the rule was that any fish could be caught with a minimum of equipment as long as you had a maximum of patience.

So, I arrived at the Hope Bay wharf with a made-in-Hong-Kong line and a smile.

My equipment included a hook, a piece of silk thread, a devilishly clever-looking red wooden bobber, one lead pellet, and a wooden frame to wrap the whole mess around. Total investment: twenty-five cents.

"What are you going to do with that?" the fish expert asked. "Sew up your pants?"

I withheld the rapier-like response that sprang instantly to my tongue. Rather than humble him with my barefoot-boy cheek, I ran along the dock and began to jig the rig, or rig the jib, whichever it is.

"Ever fish from a sailboat before?" the expert enquired, glancing proudly at the keen, slim lines of the twenty-foot craft.

"I do it all the time," I said sagely. "I've even sailed from a fishboat."

I pulled the wrong halyard and raised the jib; the sail filled and the bow swung into a broad reach before finally responding to the tiller.

"Well done!" the owner shouted. "Now come back to the dock and pick me up."

After neatly missing a fifty-foot power cruiser with a crew of eight, all on deck and watching, I slid in along the dock, giving the expert just enough time to leap aboard.

"Sail before?" he gasped. "Only in the bathtub," I said. "Ready about! Helms Alee!" the expert shouted above the wind and the flap to the sails. He pushed the tiller towards the boom and the boom addressed itself to the back of my head.

"So that's the boom," I said, as the booming in my head subsided.

In a few dazed moments we had whipped down Plumper Sound and around the tip to South Pender Island. I had only brief glimpse of lamb bones bleaching in the sun—remnants of a first of July Saturnalia on Saturna Island.

At Gowland Point we ran into action.

"There goes a big fish," I said.

"There goes a killer whale," the expert said.

"There goes my breakfast," I said.

We were in Haro Strait in the midst of the whaling lanes where the big, black killers tease each other, make love and scare the hell out of American boaters on their way to the government check point at Bedwell Harbor.

These big mammals, their dorsal fins thrashing the water and making sounds like cannon fire, are a tourist attraction of rare value.

How I longed to watch them close-up. Through binoculars. From the safety of land.

Plunging, the whales looked like elevators dropping from the fortieth floor. Emerging, they were like the U.S.S. *Nautilus* nuclear submarine coming up for air.

Other boats in our vicinity stopped to give the whales the right of way. The whales took the right of way anyway.

The fishing expert kept up a running commentary on how to trim the sails and other useless chatter.

"The whales are here because there must be a good school of salmon around," he yelled.

"Slack the main sheets," he said. "And let's do some fishing." The wind had dropped to zilch as the expert baited his line and cast.

His expensive line sank again and again into the sea. My Chinese hook, line and stinker fought a short, unmemorable encounter with my sweater—and lost. It lay in a miserable, tangled heap on the deck.

The whales continued to leap around us, nuzzling each other shamelessly and making complete fools of themselves. The expert's comment that they seldom, if ever, upset boats on purpose, calmed me not at all.

Since my fishing gear was inoperable, it was my task to keep the boat on course, sailing it gently into the wind. I lined the sails up with a piece of tattered bunting that flew from somewhere in front of the boat. Despite my inexperience, I felt I was doing grandly.

Then the expert said: "Watch that jib. You're luffing badly."

A cruel, unnecessary remark. I may not be much of a sailor or fisherman. But if there's one thing I pride myself on it's my luffing.

Chapter Thirteen
MALCONTENT IN A TENT

*In which it is pointed out that most women campers
wouldn't touch Omar with a tent pole.*

Camping in the Gulf Islands has become an institution. As an inmate of that particular institution, I feel qualified to point out some of camping's hidden cultural merits.

Among campers, as among other homo saps, there are distinct classes, in this case, the upper and lower births. "High Camp" refers to those posh trailer types whose carriages are so complete that their owners have no need to go anywhere at all to have a home away from home. In fact, some *don't* go away at all. They just send the trailer and wait until it comes back with a full report.

Second rung on the camp ladder holds the camper truck enthusiasts. Not quite as grand as the Airstreams, the Winnie-

Baggos and others of that ilk, the truckers can still pack in most of the amenities of the suburbs with them.

More and more of these muscle jobs are taking over the campsites, arriving around three o'clock, depositing a thermos bottle and a brace of folding chairs in the best spots, and then heading into town to the pub.

However, in this chapter we are dealing with the *Low Camp Creature*: The Tent Caperpillar.

This fuzzy-mouthed object can be seen in camp and out wherever disasters are found. See her emerging from the laundromat or service station washroom, kid-laden and drip-dried.

Needless to say, most camp followers are men; women are reluctantly along for the ride. Show me a woman who really enjoys tenting and I'll show you a battered wife.

Wives and sweethearts are keenly aware of the obvious distinction between the dream girl in color coordinates emerging from the Home On Wheels and the dust-covered nightmare crawling out of a tent.

At Mouat Park on Salt Spring we talked to a perverse male tenter who waved contemptously at a nearby mobile home: "You couldn't get me into one of those things if you paid me," he said.

His wife, arthritic from sleeping on the ground for twenty years, kicked at him with her one good leg and said: "I'll make you an offer you can't refuse."

Nevertheless, tenting has advantages which are not immediately discernible to the uninitiated (a polite way of saying "snobs").

For example, the ancient and revered art of Soap-Carving is a result of tent-camping. It owes its recent revival almost exclusively to tenters who have repeatedly thrown their lemon-fresh Spree into the ashes along with the water.

There are others:

CREATIVE CLOTHES HANGING: "Creative" describes the language forthcoming from him after he hits the clothes line at neck level while seeking a shortcut to the privy. It also describes her language after the line, sodden with sunshine brightness, gives a lusty twang and plops into the muck.

ROCK INDENTIFICATION: Rockhounds please take note. Here is your chance to give close scrutiny to rare geological orders when your cot collapses at midnight and deposits you on your sub-strata.

ASTRONOMICAL BEARINGS: You have the great opportunity to chart your life through the Constellations while examining stars and planets through a hole punched in the tent roof while setting the thing up in a blinding rainstorm.

FAMILY TOGETHERNESS: The wonderful enjoyment of pitching in together for the common good. Helpful son cuts up wooden tent pegs for kindling while Dad looks for something to tie tent down with. Later, Dad ties Son to tree while he cuts more tent pegs. Meanwhile, Mother can be counted upon to find other camper's missing tent pegs which are cleverly concealed in the ground all around the campsite. Her joyful shouts cheer the woods for miles.

TEEPEE CRAWLING: This used to refer to something the Indians did while waiting for the deer and the antelopes to stop playing. It now refers to fellow-travellers. At one campsite on the Gulf Islands a California woman came over to tell us about her latest operation. She sat down on our forty-nine cent Goodwill camp chair and gesticulated wildly, a tea cup in one hand and a giant filter tip cigarette in the other. The canvas seat suddenly ripped at the middle seam and deposited the matron, ash over tea cup, into some prickle bushes. It is apparent from her response that she was a veteran of the Tent Circuit. Her language was as colorful as any sideshow barker. My wife added two words to her vocabulary! Another bonus for tenters!

SOCIAL INTERCOURSE: Refers to making friends with fellow campers. Any sort of intercourse is impossible. We did however have a brief interlude before the family expanded. On our honeymoon we acquired a sleeping bag which was large enough so it gave the illusion of flight and pursuit. But the mosquitoes found us even there.

Chapter Fourteen
BEANS AND SQUARES

*In which it is shown that a Gulf Islander who does not
give two toots for Boston, will square off at
the drop of a bean.*

Gourmets from Boston, Mass., to Boston Bar, B.C., have
extolled the baked bean as a "wonderful fruit." And the good
people of the Gulf Islands have taken several notes.

Every year they mop, dust, fumigate and beautify the in-
teriors of certain old community halls and announce that for
one night only, Bean is King.

More than three hundred such bean lovers advance
yearly on Beaver Point Hall on Salt Spring Island to work
their way through a mountain of beans, cole slaw, coffee and
pie. The air is pungent with the smell of beans, cleaning

fluid, old vee-joint and an alarming number of small children for whom no parents can be found.

Dress for all Island functions ranges from haute to low couture, that is, from mink stoles to gumboots—and, in some cases, both on the same person. Beaver Point is no different.

After beaning themselves to death at the tables, Salt Springers and their friends take their places at benches around the room and watch their neighbors fork themselves into oblivion.

When the last bean has been tucked into a cavity somewhere, the dishes are pried off the tables and skidded into the dark area known as the kitchen. Here, galley slaves, engaged for the evening, stare balefully at an incredible mess of unwashed dishes and at the bean eaters still waiting to be served, and fling the remains back into the pot for next year.

One old Salt Springer told me that the secret to the Beaver Point beans, that is their tenderness and succulence, relies upon a secret remedy. "We place rocks in the pot with the beans," she said, "and when the rocks become soft, we throw away the beans and serve the rocks."

Which accounts for the stoned look on the faces of the bean-feeders.

The other event that keeps the Gulf Island halls jumping higher than Mexican jumping beans is the annual square dance socials.

A square dance caller, whose mother was obviously scared by a radio announcer with the croup, mounts the podium, clothed only in a Western hat, a giant microphone and a recording of Marvin Rainwater singing "Where the deep and pearly water."

He announces redundantly that the first square is about to begin and then clears his throat. The sound is amplified four hundred times until it resounds like a Boeing 707 with a dirty mind leaving Seattle for the last time.

Several bats leave the belfry in alarm.

The music screeches into a lively reel and the caller adds a few comments in a foreign langauge and in connection with the national political scene: "Allemande Left!: This obviously has to do with the Socialist movement in Germany. "Dosey Doe", is a reference to Bambi during a sleepy moment in Disneyland.

Dancers in old clothes careen off in opposite directions to their partners until they run into each other at various dark corners and fights break out.

This action continues until Marvin Rainwater's "Pearly Waters" wears out, or, if there is a live band, the fiddler dies.

At no point, however, does the square dance caller stop talking, singing along with Marvin, or humming to the remaining bats.

He may, however, as happened at the last square dance we attended, stop long enough to lower the music to slightly above the pain threshold to admonish several gentlemen for wearing short sleeves.

"The ladies don't like to grab on to a hairy arm, he boomed.

I completely disagreed with him. My lady partner possessed the hairiest arm I'd ever seen, and grabbing hold of it was mightly handy as I fought my way around those darn Dosey Doses.

Chapter Fifteen
WITHOUT THE REMOTEST CONTROL

An American ferry tale about a misguided tour.

As the *Vesuvius Queen* ferry bore down on his stalled pleasure craft last week, Herman Klugg thought for sure he had run afoul of the Flying Dutchman, the legendary ghost frigate.

"Frigate!" Klugg yelled, or something to that effect, as the mist-concealed ship headed straight for his disabled boat.

Klugg, from Bremerton, Washington, was on his way to Campbell River to pick up his commercial canning equipment after making his forty-seventh consecutive trip to Seattle to sell the sport salmon he had canned during the summer.

Unable to avoid collision, Klugg held on to his aft and was flipped like a kipper aboard the ferry.

Although the entire area was shrouded with its usual mist, plus a generous donation of crud from the Crofton pulp mill, Klugg knew instinctively that he was alone. The only person aboard.

He was found a few minutes later, raving and demanding fresh water when the ferry docked at Vesuvius.

At this point, a man who looked like the Ancient Mariner gave him artificial repiration and a real albatross for his neck.

Another man in white hat and blue unifrom demanded double fare. After checking his fee schedule the officer declared the boat a motor vehicle and—although he was lying on his face—classified Klugg as a foot passenger.

It did Klugg no good whatever to plead for half-fare simply because he got on the ferry halfway across the channel. Ferrymen are sticklers for the rules.

If it hadn't been for this little incident, goodness knows how long it would have been before anyone found out that during slack periods the *Vesuvius Queen* makes trips without a living person aboard. And that includes the crew.

An inquiry was ordered and evidence was produced which showed the captain had worked out an ingenious automatic pilot system.

The raw materials were simple: a handful of elastic bands, a Klondike Kate garter, two fruit jar rings and a hairpin.

The ferry would twaddle across the Stuart Channel at its usual one and one-quarter knots and strike the landing pier dead on.

The elastic bands would expand from the gunwales with the impact and drop and raise the drawbridge. The fruit jar rings would twang out and lift the barrier on the dock and then drop it immediately if anyone was foolish enough to try to get under it and onto the ferry.

The Klondike Kate garter would whip off and turn the green light red, flip the hairpin into reverse, and the ferry would go back empty.

At the end of the shift the oiler would come aboard the *Vesuvius Queen*, sprinkle some ashes on the floor, rub Bon Ami on his white hat and exchange Horatio Hornblower books with the engineer. Things looked bad for the ferry personnel.

The hearing into charges brought against the ferrymen also inferred that they had been spending all their time playing basketball in front of the Vesuvius Hotel.

This was judged to be a lie. The Ancient Mariner (who was so old that he could remember when the hotel restaurant was open), said power lines near the hotel made it impossible to get away a good, clean centre shot.

Besides, he said, sea gulls kept sitting on the basketball hoop, so volleyball was the name of the game.

A ferry official from Victoria also defended the Salt Spring crew's actions. He said there wasn't enough business during the off-season to warrant any better service than was being provided.

He said he had personally taken a nose count the preceding week and discovered an average of four cars, a school teacher on a scooter and an old lady pushing three hippies in a wheelbarrow.

The official also threatened it might be necessary to return to the former Arabian Navy schedule that was invoked once before when business waned. The schedule came into effect right after the Four Day War between Egypt and the

Israelis and ran thusly: ferry crossings every half-hour at lunchtime Tuesdays; hourly when the stores in Duncan were closed; dangerous cargo on Friday and Never On Sunday.

However, the schedule was changed after W. A. C. Bennett (who was then Premier of the Province) became extremely displeased because he was delayed in getting over to his summer residence in Vesuvius Bay.

The outcome of the case proved that the crewmen were neglectful of their duties and each was fined 85 cents, to be deducted from their twenty-three dollar a week wage. And the Bon Ami was confined to the washbowls and heads for two months.

Chapter Sixteen
I SPY WITH MY LITTLE EYE

*In which a small screen critic scans big screen movies
on a small screen.*

I miss the movie spectaculars they used to show in the community halls on the Gulf Islands.

When a really big-screen movie came to the little hall, much of the stereofrantic, orthopedic, wrap-around sound and color was lost to the walls and ceilings because it was too big and powerful for the flat eight-foot screen and one loud-speaker.

That is, they had lots of Cinema, but not much Scope.

Take for example the last movie I saw as Fulford Hall. It was billed as "The Biblical Spectacular to end all Biblical Spectaculars." It was the life story of God.

During one of the many miracles performed on the screen, the power failed. The tone of the movie tended to go downhill. However, it picked up again when someone in a back row said, in a sepulchural voice, "Let There Be Light!"

And there was light. And the movie went on. And on. And on.

Most Cinemascope spectaculars tend to run about four hours. That's about three hours too long when you're sitting on straight-backed wooden chairs.

Two boys visiting from Calgary sat through a Western double-feature on Pender Island. One boy suffered severe saddle sores from roughing it on the chairs. The other one had to have surgery to remove one of the rungs from his backside.

But the most exciting night at the movies for me was when they showed Tom Jones, the sexy English show that starts off with a great, wild hunt scene.

So much of the movie slopped off the little flat screen onto the walls and celing that two local dogs were run down and a young girl from Fernwood was ravished by the onrushing huntsmen.

Another great movie I enjoyed on the little screen was The High and the Mighty, the classic airline disaster story written by Ernest K. Gann, who lives in the American Gulf Islands (the San Juans) at Friday Harbor.

Half the movie was over before I realized that there was someone else in the cockpit with John Wayne. I really thought Big John had flipped his wings and had been talking to himself.

All this time co-pilot Robert Stack was sitting there in his supportive role. But he was so far off the screen that he might just as well have been in the luggage compartment where the hostesses hold their parties.

The sound was something else too. It was also *somewhere* else. Instead of twelve speakers, wall-to-wall realism creating the sound of mighty pistons throbbing across the sky, it was exhaust fumes from the projector and the sounds of mice eating in the adjoining kitchen.

Regardless of the screen restrictions, the audience was attentive. They felt the airplane—whenever it disappeared off the pint-sized screen—was just a wing and a prayer from crashing into the folding chairs.

No phony special effects were necessary. And audience involvement was genuine. There was so much shooting during "O.K., Gunfight At The Corral" that one old lady went home with a bullet in the intermission.

Maybe it really was the disappointment of not being able to see more than one person on the screen at one time (half a person during closeups) that led to a decision to stop showing movies in the community halls.

In any event, they may be back if we can believe the rumors coming out of Hollywood these days.

It seems the experts down there have discovered at least two ways to show big heads on small screens. One plan is to issue extra-sensitive glasses, like the Three D spectacles, to every patron so he can distinguish actors and actresses from anything else that might be among the nightlife crawling up the walls.

Despite their shortcomings and goings, the wide-screen movies did much to wrench Gulf Islanders from their apathy towards progress and fling them into the first half of the Twentieth Century.

Who knows? Maybe if they can get the second half of the screen they may even make it into the second half of the century.

Chapter Seventeen
BACK TO THE BOTTLE HOUR

It may be good wine, but is it Goody wine?

As a salute to the many wine and beer-makers on the Gulf Islands, I respectfully submit the following *Song of the Islands*: (To be sung to that popular alcoholic dirge, Days of Wine and Roses.)

> *The wine at Dave's and Rose's*
> *Takes your breath away.*
> *It's not Beaujolais.*
> *Good odor,*
> *No bouquet.*

The reason there are so many do-it-yourself winos on the Gulf Islands is because there is only one government drunk store where you can buy the stuff legally. Therefore, Islanders have to rely on bootlegging friends or make thier own.

Fortunately the Islands once were the centre of the B.C. fruit-growing industry so there are many varieties of wine-making fruits here.

With a harvest of some sort every spring, summer and fall month, there is a continuous orgy of apple-pressing, grape-stomping, raspberry-razing and cherry-choking.

See Tarzan of the Grapes, a real swinger, with his purple feet. See Jane, her lips cherry red, from red cherries. See the Royal Canadian Mounted Police raiding the house with the still on the hill where the stags are drinking their fill.

On a clear night, one Ganges house, its occupants full of apple jack, can be heard on Galiano.

But make no mistake about it, the Island potables are positively palatable. Even the products of the less-qualified brewers and distillers would make any Newfoundlander screech.

In an effort to upgrade all Island wine and beer-making standards, Gulf Island Secondary School adult studies division decided to offer a night school course with "Goody" Goodman in charge of the vats.

The course was excellent and everyone got right into the spirit of things. Some students passed the course; others drank their failures and passed out.

But at the end of it all, the majority of the students were able to converse like connoisseurs on the subject of wine. "That's an aggressive little fellow you've got there," they would say with carefree abandon at parties, thus assuring themselves of lifelong enmity and admiration.

"Come try this one, Jack," a matron called out at a wine and cheese gathering sponsored by the Chamber of Commerce. The aroma is "devastating", she said, and would make any Chamber pale.

"Goody" of course was understandably pleased as punch with his students and, as a final gesture, decided to toss a wine-tasting party in their honor. The students were to submit a sample of their very best.

"Goody", as mentioned, was a good instructor.

He also has a reputation for making wine. He is also a practical joker. Furthermore, "Goody" is the undertaker for the Gulf Islands.

And therein lies the alcohol rub.

"Goody" cannot resist a joke for long and, although he does not take his business of laying people away lightly, he is not long-faces about the job either.

As the party progressed and everyone's spirit rose with each glass of bubbly—still or sparkling—the clamor grew louder for a sample of "Goody's" own special brew.

The mortician agreed. He whisked out of the room for a moment, then returned, holding a large bottle, the label of which he held to his chest. He poured everyone a generous portion.

A toast was chug-a-lugged and seconds called for and received.

After another round, "Goody" turned the label of the bottle around so everyone could read it: "Embalming Fluid!"

It wasn't, of course. But those who were still not too stiff to move agreed that it was a "most aggressive little fellow."

Chapter Eighteen
SHRINKING BOARDS AND OTHER DEAD WOOD

*The depths that some people on the Gulf Islands will
sink just to get a drink (of water).*

As anyone with two eyes can see, the Gulf Islands are
covered with trees and surrounded by water. Consequently,
it's hard to believe that they are short of both.

The wood shortage is particularly evident if you don't
own your own forest. Most Islanders are reluctant to cut
down tress and covet what wood they have for their fire-
places.

Despite warnings about salty beach wood corroding
chimneys and iron fire boxes, the beach is a prime source
of fuel.

So much so that a souvenir shop owner told me there isn't a good-looking piece of driftwood between South Pender and Lasqueti Island.

That other abundant commodity, water, tends to be mostly the salty kind, the sort that drove the Ancient Mariner up the yardarm. Of course, there's no telling where a good salt-free well might spring up and some people will go amazing depths to get it.

One Fruitvale Road neighbor of ours told the commercial drillers at his place—after two weeks of fruitless efforts—to take their equipment and their two salt holes and leave. The owner had no intention of going into the salt business and the holes are useless. They were so porous they would't even hold dirt.

The story had a happy ending: the neighbor discovered that a well that he had been using to water the garden with had practically an endless supply of clean, pure aqua.

Another Gulfer, this one on Wallace Island, a two-hundred acre plot between Galiano and Salt Spring, asked a commercial driller to come over and dig a number of wells. Unfortunately, after waiting for several weeks for the man to arrive, he was away when the driller floated in with his equipment on a barge.

With no one to tell him where to drill, and not wishing to tie up his equipment for any length of time, the driller plunged ahead on his own.

Wallace Island now has these neat little holes all over its logging roads that lead nowhere. Neither do the wells.

Salt Spring is the only Gulf Island that is blessed with salt springs that still burble up in places. Unfortunately, as noted elsewhere, these are not of the thermal kind and do not ease rheumatism like those at Radium Hot Springs or Banff.

But even salt water can be merchandized if placed in the right hands. The Chamber of Commerce came up with two left ones when it tried to sell the village of Ganges on promoting its claim to salt. Since there are no salt springs within a tourist's toss of the centre of town, the scheme was to drill a hole through a block of salt and run a pipe of water through that. The idea met with salty disapproval.

Meanwhile, residents of Maxwell Mountain and St. Mary Lake are worried about the receding water on what they like to think is their private supply. St. Mary Lake folks who own planes say if the water level gets any lower they may have to switch from pontoons to wheels.

Maxwell Mountaineers contend that there are foreign substances among the Ganges drinkers who might prove harmful to their lake bacteria.

But Salt Spring's problems are nothing compared with the water shortages experienced on Galiano, home of the Galiano Water Diviners.

This group worships Adam's Ale and drinks nothing stronger than settled swamp water. As a result, they've built up such immunity to fungus and bugs that whenever an old-timer leaves the Island for a trip somewhere, he is advised to take a jug of the good stuff with him.

Even with this precaution, it has sometimes been necessary in innoculate a returnee at the dock if it is apparent that he has come in contact with a dose of pure water somewhere.

Fortunately, in the water-short Gulf Islands there are still some residents who wouldn't use water if you gave it to them in a glass of Scotch.

A pensioner on Saturna is so water-shy that he makes Jeeter Lester look like Esther Williams. Lester, as you may recall, was the Erskine Caldwell character who maintained the same low regard for water as Bathless Groggins and W. C. Fields.

This old chap's morning ablutions consist of dipping two fingers into a tumbler of water and rubbling them into his eyes.

To ensure maximum cleanliness, the fingers are rotated once a month. The water is then boiled for coffee.

Such stringent control and hoarding of water may not be necessary much longer if a plan being promoted by the Agriculture Department to attract grape-growing to the Gulf Islands takes root.

Grapes make excellent wine. Wine is a liquid. After stomping the grapes to clean the feet, the liquid may— after a decent length of time—be imbibed. Get the picture? If all Islanders switch over to wine they'll save enough water to flush the Number One problem down the drain.

And after that they can go to work on the wood shortage.

Chapter Nineteen
SALT SPRING STIFF NECKS

Some residents keep a stiff upper lip while looking down their noses at those who are looking up.

Salt Spring Islanders have long been accused of snobbishness—especially by those residents of the so-called "Outer Islands": Mayne, the Penders, Saturna, Galiano, Thetis, Kuper, and so on.

This is due partly to the fact the Salt Springers have a tendency to enter a room as though they owned it.

Galiano people enter the room as though they don't care *who* owns it.

And fat, rich Mayne Islanders enter a room confident in the knowledge that if one of them doesn't own it *now*, one of them soon will.

At any rate, Salt Spring residents lately have had their noses even higher in the air than usual. The reason: UFOs, flying saucers, call them what you will.

Salt Springers have claimed in the past that they are on a UFO grid or lane that extends across the Island from Galiano and thence to Thetis and downtown Duncan. John Magor, the former newspaperman and now publisher of a magazine on UFO's, lives near Duncan and, presumably, the space visitors drop in at Magor's place on Quamichan Lake to quaff a brew before heading back to Mercury, Venus or Denver.

Meanwhile, the sightings go on. Just this week I was told by one hundred and forty-seven Islanders that they saw UFOs. In a space of four days.

Strangely, most of this stellar crockery has been observed taking off from the Beddis Park area where residents have been fighting off determined attempts by non-residents to establish a boat launching ramp.

Beddis Roaders claim the noise, confusion and pollution caused by boats will ruin the peace and privacy of public bathers.

A cynical observer pointed out that this complain doesn't hold water because the Beddis Park folk don't want public bathers either.

What has this to do with flying saucers? Simply this: It was revealed in secret conversation overheard on the ferry this week that the flying saucers spotted by one hundred and forty-seven Islanders are in fact plastic bags filled with swamp gas and set twirling on bright disks of aluminum foil impregnated with tiny, flaming candles.

The effect is startlingly real and amazingly like what one hundred and forty-seven Islanders would take to be a flying saucer. Or perhaps a birthday cake going into orbit.

The launching area of this deception? Beddis Park.

I have therefore decided it is my public duty to report this information before any more panic develops. Already real estate values have dropped drastically in the Beddis area and plans to build a launch ramp have been grounded.

Excuse me. The count of UFO sightings on the Island has gone up. I just spoke to another Islander.

AHA... THIS DEFINITELY CALLS FOR A TURPENTINE ENEMA!

Chapter Twenty
THE KILLING CURES

It is said that Gulf Islanders live longer than anyone else. It may just seem longer.

Non-residents of the Gulf Islands constantly marvel at the fact that people on the Gulf Islands seem to go on living forever.

A good example was "Granny" Stark, a former plantation slave and one of Salt Spring's best-loved pioneers, who died a few years ago at one hundred and six. She was a tough one.

So was a certain Doctor Lockhart who lived near Cusheon Lake. He successfully applies for a free punching bag from the firm who supplied him with the original because he claimed he had outlived the "lifetime guarantee" on the bag.

A man living on Prevost Island used to row across to Ganges to get his heart medicine, much to his doctor's consternation. The old chap finally had to give it up. His doctor died from a bad heart.

Of course there may be some exaggerations. Such as the story of the old chap on North Galiano whose liver was so healthy that six days after he died at the age of one hundred and four the liver was still working and had to be beaten to death with a stick.

The reasons for the marvelous longevity of the Islanders has been speculated upon from time to time and I am happy to say that speculation time is here again.

I am indebted to a Gulf Islands woman for this well-researched information on Gulf Islands remedies for what ails you, taken from several well-thumbed journals.

According to the information, it is sulphur and molasses that keeps everyone healthy, regardless of whether it is rheumatism or Spring Fever that is causing the upset. The theory must be that S & M is good for something, because it tastes so *bad*.

Since colds were prevalent then as now, a whole section was devoted to curing that pesky affliction. "For a cold, a drink of lemon juice, honey and flax seed, boiled and taken very hot is very good," one recipe reads.

A teaspoonful of baking soda dissolved in a glass of cold water and taken every four hours will check a cold, it says here. However, a notation in the margin oberves: "It never stopped the cold for me—but it sure got something else going!"

A chest rub was made by taking "two parts of lard, one part turpentine and one part coal oil. Rub the mixture on the affected area."

I don't know about that "affected area", but a person could get burned just standing next to somebody smeared like that. Put that guck on a Channel swimmer and you'd soon have a world speed record.

Of course, the cures were for more than just colds. One remedy for sciatica recommended grinding a garlic clove into a pair of old socks. The sufferer was to wear the socks "day and night for three weeks for quick relief."

Unfortunately it did not offer any "relief" for the person forced to share the same house, room or bed with the sufferer.

Burns and scalds, according to the medical journal, could be healed with a poultice of raw potato or cold tea leaves; blisters by a poultice of warm water and linseed meal.

Like the man who had a mustard plaster with a built-in hotdog, the patient could at least think about food while he was waiting for his wounds to get healed.

Despite improving medical service and establishment of treatment centres like the Coleman Clinic on Pender Island, warding off sickness is still easier for a Gulf Islander than getting to hospital.

So is it any wonder that they live so long and seem so healthy? With remedies like these to look forward to, they're just plain terrified to get sick.

CHAPTER TWENTY-ONE
THE TOASTING OF RED HOWARD

Red Howard said it was the greatest day of his life when
they toasted him at the Mayne Island Inn. Meanwhile,
the artist who did the portrait had her face fried
in Vancouver.

Beer flowed like champagne at the Mayne Island Inn, the
renovated brick worker's hostel, the night Red Howard un-
veiled his own portrait.

Red, with his fine Irish, born-in-Chemainus brogue,
stood up to the cheers of his fellow Mayneliners and toasted
himself. He also toasted the artist, but he needn't have both-
ered.

Donna Farrell, the lovely lass who painted the portrait of
Red, already had enough toastiness to last her for life. She'd

fallen asleep under a sunlamp and couldn't get over to Mayne for the unveiling.

Considering the fact that Miss Farrell had never met the old fisherman (she did the painting from a color photograph), it was an amazing likeness. Trouble was, the old boxer didn't look a bit like himself that night.

Whereas the portrait showed him in his usual garb of shirt sleeves, winter underwear showing at the neck and a wiry beard, there he stood in a business suit and a shave. Hardly anybody knew him.

"Sure, it's me," he told everyone as the congratulations came on. "Look at them eyebrows." "Those eyes belong to a kind man," Miss Farrell is reported to have said of the weather-beaten, ring-smashed, craggy old sockets.

The wrinkles around Red's eyes, once begun, traced a southern course to his fists, as he would point out at the drop of a glass.

"See these hands?" Red said. "The doctor said I had arthritis. Hell, that ain't arthritis. I busted 'em up so much when I was in the ring that they never got time to heal before it was time to fight again.

Red's prowess with his hams was only surpassed by his love for a well-filled jug, and both got a workout one afternoon when a police boat spotted his fishboat drifting aimlessly in Active Pass.

The way Red told it to me the police boat stopped and an officer hopped aboard to enquire if the captain would care to steer a straight course in preference to the circles he was making.

Seems the wash was causing some Islanders to fear for their docks; also, there was something said rather strongly about a ferry or two wanting to get through the Pass without splitting a seam.

Red saw red and threw the officer overboard. Reinforcements thudded into the little fishboat and the old brawler was finally subdued. "It was a grand fight," Red recalled.

The best story about Red Howard that I know concerns the hair-raising episode in which he threatened to hang himself because a certain lady named Sophie wouldn't (or couldn't) share his undying devotion.

Smitten, smote and damn near smothered with affection, emotion and other stimulants, Red climbed onto an orange crate, threw a rope over a rafter and tied the other end around his sinewy neck.

He was all poised for the awful moment in which life would end and he would be found all strung up like a Christmas goose—pinfeathers and all.

The suspense was tremendous.

Finally, he reached up and cut the rope with his pocketknife.

It was speculated upon that Red couldn't bear facing a rerun of his life that would most certainly stream past his eyes like a crazy movie in those last moments of consciousness.

Others said he thought he heard the telephone ring and figured it might be the lady in question, Sophie, full of remorse and love.

But Red wouldn't have any part of either explanation.

"Shucks," he said, "it wasn't anything like that. I just decided no woman on earth was worth that kind of sacrifice."

Chapter Twenty-Two
A CROSSWALK OF ANIMALS

For those who want to know the real reason for the chicken crossing the road.

The world's first crosswalks exclusively for the use of animals will be built on the Gulf Islands.

A group known as Animal Savers Socety (ASS, for short, made the announcement this week following an economic boycott.

"We had to do something," an ASS official said. "It was getting so bad that it wasn't safe for a chicken to cross the road."

.

Drivers leaving the ferries were accused of speeding around curves at fifteen and twenty miles an hour and not allowing rightaway to deer, cattle and sheep that stroll leisurely from one shoulder of the road to the other.

An ASS representative testified that reports of pigs hogging the highway and trucks having to hit the ditches because vagrant bovines wanted to lock horns with them was "grossly inaccurate."

"Such assinine remarks made us resolve to take the bull by the tail and not count our chickens before they bite the hand that feeds them," the official said, mixing his metaphors madly.

He further complained that many choice areas of pasture along the roads and ditches had been ruined by cars and trucks rolling over on them after they swerved to avoid animals on the road.

The ASS decided to do something about this danger to the animals.

"For too long we have been gamboling with our lives," said a spring lamb from Saturna.

A strike was imminent after the ASS turned down a last minute suggestion by cattle that cars driving Gulf Island roads be equiiped with cow-catchers, the way locomotives are.

"Cow-catchers are fine," the official said, "but what of the squabs and piglets, to say nothing of the dogs and peahens."

Another suggestion that farmers be required to maintain fences alondside their roadside acreage or be faced with a "pound law" was vetoed by the Island farmers.

"We've got enough to do lobbying Victoria for higher milk and feed prices and Ottawa for lower taxes on equipment and better freight rates without having to look after a bunch of cows and horses," the farmers said.

A mediator was called in. Dr. Hiram Cheep, author of "Feed Mink By Hand" (and the sequel, "Three Fingers in the Mash"), was unable to draw any conclusions.

After being closeted with the animals for fourteen hours he had trouble even drawing his breath.

"They had some very strong points," Dr. Cheep said, especially the goats!"

After the collapse of negotiations and the negotiator, the animals decided to take things into their own hands. All but the cows, of course, who abstained because of udder considerations.

An economic boycott was begun.

Sheep refused to appear in advertisements like: "Have you ever seen a bald sheep?" Turkeys refused to dance and at Rod and Gun Club turkey shoots.

Other fowl tactics were employed: roosters confirmed they were not chicken and ordered their hens not to lay anything but down. Ducks refused to deliver down, but gave up instead. Cats caterwauled and canines had Dog Days.

Finally, pushed to the barn wall, the human residents of the Gulf Islands relented and animal crosswalks were ordered built every three or four miles.

Complete with flashing lights, level-crossing style drop bars, cattle guards and bells, these devices will be manned day and night—by humans.

An invitation has been sent to the Minister of Agriclture to attend a ribbon-cutting ceremony at the opening of the first crosswalk.

The ASS had planned to top the occasion with a human sacrifice but this was frowned upon by a number of animalitarians, the animal equivalent of humanitarians.

But not without an argument from the meaphorical ASS man. "I think they should get the raw end of the sacrificial lamb for once," he said.

Chapter Twenty-three
GARBAGE ON THE HIGH SEAS

Or how pitching and tossing got the seas so high in the first place.

It was a perfect day for a launching: Wind, calm; Sea, light chop, moderate swell; Sky, blue, cloudless.

The old lady gingerly removed a grey bundle from the back seat of her automobile, glanced furtively around to make sure the coast was clear, and then hoisted the package over the ferry rail.

Plop! Another successful burial at sea.

Gulf Islanders have developed one of the largest, best-organized disposal systems in the world: garbage-dumping by hand from the B.C. Ferries.

Islanders are not, by nature, polluters. But here are a few examples of true stories told to me by the Islanders themselves:

A Portland man was visiting his brother on North Pender and as he was getting ready to leave the relative asked him if he would "drop a few things" on his way home. He meant six week's garbage.

But the visitor forgot to take the cargo out of his trunk for three months. He's now in the market for a good car deodorant.

A man who lives quietly on one of the rocky Outer Islands hasn't enough earth on his atoll to cover a beer cap; consequently he suffers from bottle fatigue once a year when he has to row out in the Strait and sink his empties one by one.

A Fulford Harbor matron told me she was mortified to learn what happened to the well-wrapped parcel she intended to donate to the gulls on the way to Sidney. She mailed her sister the throwawys and threw her Christmas present overboard in its place.

The proprietor or a store at Port Washington on Pender Island used to watch with mixed emotions each evening as a little old lady customer sneaked down to add her daily rations of garbage to his trash barrel.

A marine operator at Browning Harbor said he wasn't worried though about the yachtsmen who spill their swill from the poop decks.

"If anything," he said, "the fish are getting fatter around here."

Another example of hope for the future is the old codger who used to fling his slops off the Port Washington pier.

When I suggested to him that statistics proved that all that crap would be back on his own beach in five years, he said: "Five years, you say? Well . . . let's see now. I'm sixty-seven years old and statistics prove that I won't be around then to welcome it."

An unfortunate ferryman was enlisted by an Islander to dispose of a rusting automobile by dumping it from the ferry at sea. The wreck ended up in a fisherman's net. The Mounties traced the owner through the serial number on the engine block.

The owner confessed and the poor ferrymen got a suspension and a fine, thus ending what could have become a unique but expensive Island beautification program.

What can Islanders do except get down in the dumps about their garbage situation? There are very few pickup services. Besides, as with most things, Islanders would rather suffer a bit of inconvenience than an increase in taxes.

Ferryland's motto is "Death Before Taxes."

Another factor of course is the danger of fire; until the fire season is over most Islanders have to live with their leftovers.

It's this period, not Dominion Day on July First, that people on Saturna speak of when they say they are having a high time.

While researching this article by eavesdropping on travelers on the *Mayne Queen*, I was suddenly bombed by a badly-thrown carton of peelings and coffee grounds.

As I stood there, wreathed in grounds with a banana peel slithering down my shoulder, one old chap remarked: "Nothing like adding a little local color, I always say!"

Chapter Twenty-four
HARBOR HOUSE WENT SWIMMINGLY ALONG

*Entertainment was supplied by the guests, whether they
knew it or not.*

It is an unfortunate fact of life that during the past few
years the most interesting hotels on the Gulf Islands have had
a bad habit of burning themselves down. At this writing, the
Vesuvius Hotel was latest to disappear in a shower of sparks;
old Harbor House and a rustic veteran on Galiano had already bit the dust.

Mayne Island has hung onto its accommodation since
new owners turned an old brick-makers hostel into an accept-
able Inn.

Harbor House was started shortly after Fred Crofton arrived on Salt Spring in 1899 and learned how to farm from

fellow-Irishman John Scovell who sold him his one hundred acre property in 1904.

The guest house began while Fred was away at war in 1914 and it became a rambling storey after that. From the livingroom the business grew and grew until it spread into a couple of wings and looked as though it might fly away.

So many guests began coming to the Island the Croftons had to build wooden-floored tents to accommodate them all.

With a piano in the second dining room, many guests supplied their own entertainment. Others *were* the entertainment.

Like the little old lady who startled the other hotel guests by coming downstair in her bathing suit to dramatize that she had burst a pipe upstairs. That is, a pipe had burst in her room.

She was followed by Stanley Critchley, a longtime resident of the hotel, carrying an umbrella. Both were closely followed by a waterfall that cascaded into the lobby.

Over the years the same Stanley Critchley endeared himself to the dining room staff because of his unwavering daily schedule which began at 10 a.m. when he wound the dining room cuckoo clock. He then began a leisurely scan of the menu.

He'd fly into a rage if the waitress denied him his right to selection, even though he ordered the same thing every day: mush and a couple of poached eggs.

Every evening old Stan would be back, precisely at 10, to wind the cuckoo clock again and make himself a cup of tea. His schedule never varied in forty years.

Not that all Harbor House visitors stayed that long. But even up until recently, some were still supplying the entertainment. Particularly the film crew who came onto the Island to do some scenes for a movie called "The Blast."

The director was a three-hundred pound sight in a purple suit. Other members of the professionals staying at the Harbor House included two chaps who entered the usually staid public house in a blaze of color.

I attempted to interview these worthies with their flailing wrists covered with diamond cufflinks and fingers full of rings. It was like trying to talk to Don Quixote's windmill.

One chap was wearing a diamond stickpin in his flowered cravat and a plume in his beret. He had on eye makeup; either that or a pair of centipedes had crawled onto his elelids and died there.

While I was attempting to get in a question about how they planned to film a dramatic scene of death and adventure on Maxwell Mountain, a waiter hovered over their arms, which by now had assumed the proportions of crazed helicopter blades.

The waiter, who looked like Broderick Crawford in one of his ugliest moods, doubled during the week as a Caterpillar operator. He stood there in his white shirt, stained with beer and agape at the belly, showing off a generous expanse of hair, and waited for the flapping to stop. It never did.

His eyes were fozen open in disbelief. In his forty-odd years he had never seen anything quite like this.

"You, uh, gents, want a round here?" he grunted.

"Well, certainly dear, we'll take the whole *tray*," one individual said. "And have one for yourself, sweetie," added the one with the centipedes. He rolled his eyes and one of the crawlers fell off his face and into his beer.

I decided to call the interview off for the day; the shuffleboard game in the corner of the pub was stalled and every patron in the place was eyeballing our little coterie.

I hadn't the right flip of the wrist to feel quite at home. Besides, my throat was sore from trying to speak four octaves below normal.

However, I did call the man in the purple suit to dicuss an advertisement he had been running in the local weekly. It requested extras to work in the film.

"We've had nothing but trouble," he complained. "They just won't work. And the weather won't cooperate. It's either raining or so hot these Islanders won't get off their pratts and fight. I want action. I want action!"

Ironically, it was the burly waiter who finally came to the rescue of the film-makers and their reluctant stars.

"You want to make them dummies run around the mountain like scared sheep, right?" he asked.

"That's precisely it, my good fellow," the director in purple told the waiter in beer stains.

The waiter then whispered something in the director's ear and headed back to his job of swabbing beer off the table and into the patron's laps.

I never found out what the secret of making the Islander extras move so fast was until after the company had packed up and gone—their production segment safely in the can.

I dropped by the pub and asked the waiter-cat operator what it was that he told the director that prompted such spirited cooperation from the locals.

"I told him the only way you'd get those guys to move their tail would be to give them something worth moving for. Since they were only paying two-fifty an hour they weren't going to move very fast in this heat.

"So we went up there on the mountain and hid about a dozen cases of beer. And when the purple guy told those Salt Springers about it, they damn ripped the mountain apart trying to find it!"

Chapter Twenty-Five
SALT SPRING ROUNDABOUT

In which it is noted that progress may not be the best way to go ahead.

There is a terrific "circus" in Ganges, Salt Spring Island, that is supposed to be patterned after the famous circuses in London. But Ganges' circus owes more to Barnum and Bailey than to Picadilly or St. Giles.

The traffic intersection used to feature a World War I cenotaph right smack in the middle of the road. Drivers had the choice of turning right or left or, if you felt patriotic, driving right through it and opening up a New Front.

The local Chamber of Commerce decided the left-right-center maze was not complicated enough so they brought in an engineer fresh from an institution where he had been designing torture tests for rats.

The design he came up with for Ganges earned him another nomination for an extensive tour of duty on the funny farm. It had every modern street inconvenience: No Entry; No Exit; One Way; crosswalk arrows pointing every which way; Yield; Stop, and Crash!

After a week in operation, the service station attendant across the road remarked: "It's like musical chairs. First one to get hit has to move out."

Even as he spoke, a man drove the wrong direction up a one-way lane, then turned around and drove the wrong way down another; a woman drove past a stop sign without pausing; another woman driver stopped at the yield sign, looked both ways and plowed through a crosswalk loaded with kids and sheep.

At the time the Ganges crosswalk was opened to the public my wife was taking driving lessons from a near-sighted veteran of the Boorish War. His only concession to other traffic was to attack with his cane anyone attempting to share the road with his ancient Ford.

The old vet approached the new traffic maze with characteristic zeal: muffler flying and muffler smoking.

He got locked into a cunning combination of yield, stop and pointing arrows and around and around he went like Major Bowes' Wheel of Fortune. Finally, a rubber band holding the crank shaft exploded and the old wreck of a car stalled in a crosswalk.

When a gentleman rushed up to try to revive my wife, who was suffering from exhaust fumes and exhaustion, he was felled by a single blow from the old vet's cane.

They'd be there still if the driver hadn't got out to chase a young punk who'd leaned on the fender.

A little old lady came along and drove my wife home on the handlebars of her bike.

BACKWORD

More stories of the Gulf Islands are being written every day—by the people who act in them: the Islanders themselves. Like the man who lives with two wives and the woman who has two husband's, or the equivalent.

Or the Fulford couples who played whist together and decided each liked their opposite number better—so they switched married partners. And the whist game went on just as before, only better.

Various Islanders have run off the various other Islanders; some returned—and life went on. And goes on.

And that's the truth!